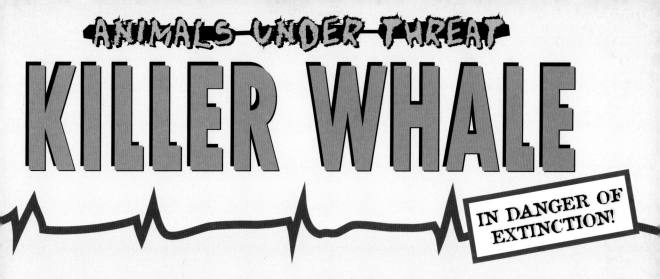

ANIMALS UNDER THREAT

KILLER WHALE

IN DANGER OF EXTINCTION!

Carol Inskipp

Heinemann Library
Chicago, Illinois

Customer Service   888–454–2279

Visit our website at www.heinemannlibrary.com

Photo research by Laura Durman
Designed by Ian Winton and Jo Malivoire
Printed in China by WKT Company Limited

09 08 07 06 05
10 9 8 7 6 5 4 3 2 1

Library of Congress Cataloging-in-Publication Data
Inskipp, Carol, 1948-
  Killer whale / Carol Inskipp.
      p. cm. — (Animals under threat)
  Includes bibliographical references.
  ISBN 1-4034-5584-8 (hc) — ISBN 1-4034-5691-7 (pbk.)
  1. Killer whale—Juvenile literature. I. Title. II. Series.
  QL737.C432I57 2004
  599.53′6—dc22

                            2004000571

Acknowledgments
The author and publisher are grateful to the following for permission to reproduce copyright
material: ardea.com pp. 32 (F. Gohier), 39 (M. Watson); Bruce Coleman Collection/Pacific
Stock pp. **4, 8, 17, 20**; Bruce Coleman Inc. p. **43**; CORBIS pp. 27 (Neil Beer), 38 (Neil
Rabinowitz); CORBIS SYGMA p. 31 (Baril Pascal); FLPA pp. **7, 13** (F. Nicklin/Minden Pictures),
18 (G. Lacz), **23** (A. Visage), **28, 33** (T. De Roy/Minden Pictures), **36** (M. Newman); Paul
Glendell/www.glendell.co.uk p. **35**; Capt. Jim Maya, San Juan Island, WA. p. 37; NHPA pp. **25**
(Stephen Krasemann), **26** (David Currey); OSF/AA pp. **24** (Breck P. Kent), 40 (Richard Kolar);
Photodisc: cover header and background image; SeaPics.com pp. **5, 15** (A. Nachoum), **9, 19,
22, 29, 41** (I. Visser), **11, 14** (H. Minakuchi), **16** (R.L. Pitman), **30** (R.W. Baird); Still Pictures
pp. **21** (Al Grillo), **34** (Wolfgang Schmidt); WDCS, the Whale and Dolphin Conservation
Society p. **42**.

Cover photograph reproduced with permission of FLPA (G. Lacz).

Every effort has been made to contact copyright holders of any material reproduced in this
book. Any omissions will be rectified in subsequent printings if notice is given to the
publisher.

Some words are shown in bold, **like this.** You can find out what they
mean by looking in the glossary.

Contents

The Killer Whale, or Orca

Killer whales, also known as orcas, are sea animals with strong, graceful bodies boldly marked in black and white. Although they look like fish, killer whales—along with porpoises, dolphins, and other whales—are actually special kinds of **mammals** called **cetaceans.** They spend their whole lives in the water.

What are cetaceans?

Like other mammals, such as cows or humans, cetaceans are **endothermic,** or warm-blooded, and feed their young with milk. They also have lungs and need to come to the water's surface to breathe air through one or two nostrils, called blowholes.

With their striking black and white markings, orcas are among the easiest cetaceans to recognize.

Cetaceans are found in all the oceans of the world. They have torpedo-shaped bodies and powerful tails that help them swim fast through the water. They can also dive for long periods of time to great depths. Whales are generally the largest in size of the cetaceans and porpoises are the smallest.

There are two kinds of cetaceans: toothed whales and **baleen** whales. Toothed whales use their teeth to catch and hold on to **prey,** such as fish, squid, and **marine** mammals, before swallowing them whole. They have one blowhole. Killer whales, sperm whales, and all dolphins and porpoises are toothed whales.

Baleen whales, on the other hand, have no teeth. They live on very small fish, **plankton,** and other tiny living things in the ocean. Baleen is a comblike structure in the whale's mouth that filters food from the water. It is made of keratin, a material like our fingernails. Baleen whales are larger than toothed whales and have two blowholes. Blue and humpback whales are types of baleen whales.

Top predators

Playful and intelligent, killer whales are among the top **predators** in the world's oceans. This means that they hunt and eat other mammals, (including whales) as well as fish, and have no natural predators themselves, except humans. Unfortunately, like other cetaceans, killer whales face many threats today and all of these are from humans. Food shortages, **pollution** from chemicals, killing by fishers, and disturbance from boats are some of the problems that are affecting killer whales in the 21st century.

How the orca got its name

Scientists first named the killer whale in 1758. They called it *Delphinus orca* or *demon dolphin* from the Latin *delphinus* meaning "dolphin," and *orcus* meaning "lower world." It is not very clear how the killer whale name came about. It may have been because people had seen these whales attacking and killing other whales. Despite their frightening name, killer whales have not been known to attack or kill a human in the wild. The alternative name for killer whale is orca, after its modern scientific name, *Orcinus orca.*

Plates of baleen grow from the gums of humpback whales like this one. Water and food enter the mouth and the baleen strains out large numbers of tiny prey at once.

Orca Populations

Orcas live in oceans all over the world. They are some of the most widely distributed **mammals** on Earth. They can be found in warm, **tropical** seas, in cold, **polar** waters, in coastal bays, and in the open ocean. Sometimes orcas enter river **estuaries,** but they never move far from the ocean. Orcas are regular visitors around the coasts of the British Isles and all up the west coast of the United States and Canada. In Australia orcas live in the waters around Tasmania and are often seen off South Australia and Victoria.

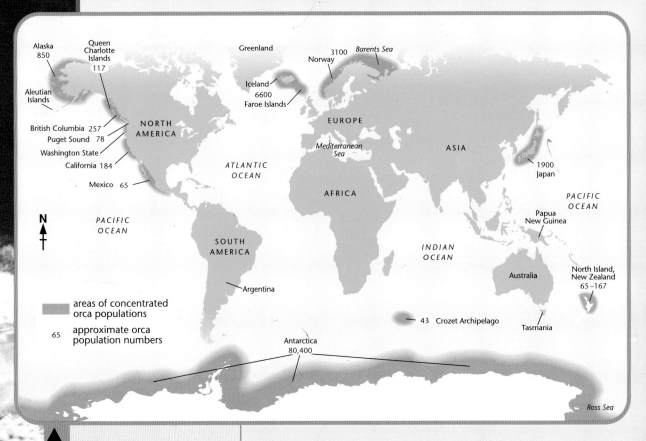

Alaska 850
Queen Charlotte Islands 117
Aleutian Islands
British Columbia 257
Puget Sound 78
Washington State
California 184
Mexico 65

NORTH AMERICA
ATLANTIC OCEAN
PACIFIC OCEAN
N

Greenland
Norway 3100
Barents Sea
Iceland
Faroe Islands 6600
EUROPE
Mediterranean Sea
AFRICA
ASIA
1900 Japan
PACIFIC OCEAN
Papua New Guinea

SOUTH AMERICA
Argentina

INDIAN OCEAN
Australia
North Island, New Zealand 65–167
Tasmania

areas of concentrated orca populations

65 approximate orca population numbers

43 Crozet Archipelago

Antarctica 80,400

Ross Sea

▲ *Orcas are found throughout the world's oceans, but are concentrated where there are rich sources of food. Unlike some whales, they do not make long journeys.*

Because orcas live in all the world's oceans and spend most of their time hidden underwater, it is difficult for scientists to study them easily, or guess how large their **populations** actually are. The total world population of orcas is not yet known, but it is possible that there are around 94,000 animals.

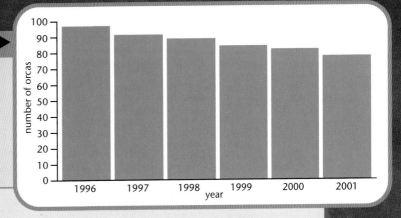

The southern resident population of orcas in Puget Sound, off the state of Washington, declined in number by 20 percent in the 6 years before 2001.

Chart: number of orcas by year

year	number of orcas
1996	~97
1997	~92
1998	~89
1999	~85
2000	~83
2001	~79

Threatened orcas

Despite the difficulties in studying orcas, two populations of these whales have been closely studied for around 30 years. One population lives off the northwest coast of the United States and Canada. The other lives around the Crozet Archipelago in the southern Indian Ocean. In both populations scientists have found a worrying decline in orca numbers.

In order to study the North American group of orcas more accurately, scientists divide this population into two: whales off the British Columbia coast are known as the northern **resident** group. Those living in Puget Sound, the waters off Washington state, and the coast of southern Vancouver are called the southern resident group. A survey of these whales carried out in 2001 showed that the northern resident population had stopped growing after increasing steadily for about twenty years. It was possibly even on the decline. The southern resident population had declined, but no one knows the reasons why. Along with a fall in the number of the fish that orcas eat, **pollution,** and growing disturbance from boats in the area may be the problems.

The population of orcas around the Crozet Archipelago has also declined dramatically in recent years. Numbers have fallen by more than half in just 10 years, to only 43 orcas in 2000. Ten years ago orcas in this area lived an average of 60 years, but today they generally live for less than 20 years. In the population that remains there are no young orcas and females of **breeding** age are continually dying. Food shortages and killing by fishers are possible reasons for this serious decline.

Orcas are most common in the cooler, coastal waters of the Antarctic where the waters are rich in **nutrients** and full of the animals that they like to eat.

The Orca Body

Orcas have sleek, smooth bodies that glide easily through the water. They are among the fastest **mammals** in the **marine** world and can swim up to 30 miles per hour (48 kilometers per hour). They use this great power of speed to help them catch fast-moving **prey.** The tall **dorsal fin** in the middle of the back keeps the orcas steady in the water and the **pectoral fins** on their sides are used like paddles for steering and stopping.

Although orcas can swim fast, they usually move at much slower speeds, about 2 to 6 miles per hour (3 to 10 kilometers per hour), about the same walking speed as humans.

A breath of air

Whales return to the water's surface regularly to breathe air. Before taking in a fresh breath, they blow out a column of moist air, known as a spout or blow, through their blowhole. Like other **cetaceans,** orcas have the amazing ability to control their breathing. Instead of sleeping, they rest by relaxing one half of their brain while guiding their swimming and breathing with the other half. When underwater, special muscles close the blowhole tightly to keep water out.

A comparison of cetacean sizes.

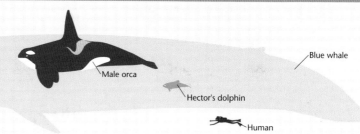

SPECIES	LENGTH	WEIGHT
Blue whale	82–102 feet (25–31 meters)	80–130 tons (80,000–130,000 kilograms)
Male orca	23–26 feet (7–8 meters)	3.6–5.5 tons (3,600–5,500 kilograms)
Female orca	16–23 feet (5–7 meters)	1.35–3.35 tons (1,350–3,500 kilograms)
Hector's dolphin	3–5 feet (1–1.5 meters)	77–143 pounds (35–65 kilograms)
Human	5½–6 feet (1.65–1.8 meters)	121–242 pounds (55–110 kilograms)

Senses

Orcas can hear a huge range of sounds. Although they have ear openings, toothed whales like the orca can receive sounds through the lower jaw. From the jaw, sounds pass to the inner ear, and finally to the brain. Orcas can see fairly well and have skin that is sensitive to touch. Like other whales, orcas have no sense of smell. We do not know whether or not they have a sense of taste.

Hot and cold

Like all **endothermic** animals, orcas need to keep their bodies at a constant temperature. Heat escapes from the body 27 times faster in water than in air. Orcas do not have fur, but like other cetaceans, they have a thick layer of fat under their skin called **blubber.** This acts as an energy store and also helps to keep them warm. Sometimes, when swimming in warmer waters for instance, orcas may become too hot. To cope with this, their large dorsal fin and tail **flukes** contain lots of blood vessels. By pumping hot blood through their fins and flukes, heat can escape more easily from the orca's body, helping it to cool off. Likewise, if an orca feels cold, it pumps as little blood as possible to these areas, and so keeps its body heat in.

Orca tears?

If you look closely at an orca's eye you will see a thick, jelly-like substance oozing out from it. The orca is not crying! This is known as the **mucus** tear and is present in all cetaceans. The mucus, which is slightly oily, helps to protect the orca's eyes and keep them clean.

Communication and Orca Groups

Orca voices

Orcas make a variety of noises, such as whistles and screams, to communicate with each other. Each orca pod has its own unique range of calls. Some calls are so distinctive that scientists can identify many of them by ear. Orcas can easily recognize their own pod from several miles away by the sounds it makes.

Orcas spend much of their time swimming around in dark, murky water. The use of sound is very important to them for finding their way around, hunting, and communicating with each other.

Echolocation

Sound travels through water more than four times faster than through air. When hunting, toothed whales like orcas use sound to tell the position of their **prey.** This is known as **echolocation.** A recent increase in underwater noise due to human activities, such as shipping and drilling for oil, might be affecting the whales' ability to use echolocation.

Orcas send out high-pitched clicking sounds and listen to differences in the echoes that return. In this way, they can build up a sound picture of their surroundings. Echolocation helps orcas to find their prey.

Sometimes pods join together for a short time to hunt, and up to 250 orcas have been seen swimming together in this way. This pod is swimming in waters off the Canadian coast.

Resident, transient, and offshore orcas

Orcas live together in family groups called **pods.** So far, scientists have discovered three distinct types of orca groups, each with different behavior: they are called the **residents,** the **transients,** and the offshores.

Resident orcas stay in their own area all the time and form closely knit family pods numbering 5 to 25 whales. They usually stay in the pod for life. Residents eat salmon and other fish that they hunt using echolocation. They call frequently to keep in touch with each other and are known to make 12 different types of sounds. Resident orcas talk to each other more than other orcas and often take part in noisy displays.

Transient orcas roam much more widely than residents, and are sometimes seen far from the shore. Their pods have weaker family ties and some orcas may leave to join other pods. Transients often form small pods of up to seven whales. They feed on any prey they can find including seals, sea lions, dolphins, and other **mammals,** as well as sea birds. Because their prey generally have good hearing, transients swim quietly and rely on surprise attacks, rather than echolocation. For this reason these groups talk to one another less often than resident orcas.

Offshore groups spend most of their time in the open water, much farther away from the shore than other orcas. Very little is known about them. Fish are probably their main **diet,** but they may eat **marine** mammals, too. Offshore orcas tend to have many scars on their fins and it is possible that they also eat sharks.

Diet and Teeth

Orcas are strong swimmers and skilled hunters. They play an important role in the **ecosystem** of the ocean. They are at the top of the **food chain**. This means that apart from humans, they have no natural **predators.**

A hearty meal!

Scientists found the remains of 13 dolphins and 14 seals in the stomach of an orca. Another orca held the remains of at least 32 adult seals!

The **diet** of orcas is the most varied of all the whales and includes several hundred different animal **species:** squid, fish, sea birds, sea turtles, seals, sea lions, penguins, and dolphins. Orcas even hunt and kill other whales. As many as 30 to 40 orcas are known to have made an attack on several hundred narwhals (unusual whales with long tusks). There are records of orcas attacking whales much larger than themselves, such as sperm whales, humpback whales, and even blue whales. Orcas have also been known to feed on land **mammals,** such as moose, that have been swept out to sea when swimming from one island to another. It is likely that the orca is the only **cetacean** that regularly kills and eats other **endothermic** animals.

Orcas have to eat a large amount of food to help keep them warm. An average-sized orca will eat 550 pounds (250 kilograms) of food a day, or 7 percent of its body weight. Young orcas, called calves, eat around 10 percent of their body weight each day because they need to grow rapidly.

Killer whale

Seal

Squid

Cod

Plant plankton

*This diagram shows how the food chain can work in the North Sea. Both food and energy are transferred up the food chain from **plankton** at the base, to the orca at the top. The arrows indicate that plankton is eaten by cod, cod is eaten by squid, and so on up the chain.*

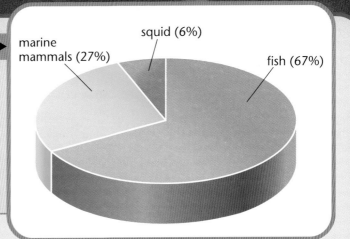

▶

Orca diets vary depending on what is available in the ocean where they live. This chart shows the type of food that makes up the diet of an orca feeding in the Antarctic Ocean.

squid (6%)

marine mammals (27%)

fish (67%)

Jaws and teeth

The orca's jaw is wide, with very powerful muscles that help it grasp large, strong **prey** that would otherwise be able to wriggle free and escape. Orca teeth curve inward and backward to help catch and grip prey tightly. Orcas use their teeth to bite and tear, but they cannot chew. They can swallow penguins and small seals whole because their throats are so huge!

Orcas have 40 to 52 sharp, conical teeth that are around 1 inch (2.5 centimeters) in diameter and nearly 3 inches (8 centimeters) long.

Tooth tales

On average, orcas in the wild live between 25 and 35 years, although they often reach 50, and some live as long as 80 years! Scientists now use orca teeth to help find out the age of these animals. As an orca gets older, it grows more and more layers on the outside of its teeth. If a section of tooth is sliced, the layers can be counted to reveal the orca's age. This is similar to telling the age of a tree by counting the rings in its trunk.

An Efficient Hunter

Orcas are highly successful **predators** that usually hunt in groups. By hunting together, orcas are also able to catch animals much bigger than themselves, although they often feed on smaller **prey.** Once a group starts hunting its prey, the animal usually has little chance of escape. As a result, the approach of orcas usually panics other **marine** life. Large male orcas often attack dangerous prey, and have even been known to attack great white sharks.

Surprise attack

Orcas use a variety of hunting techniques to catch their prey. In **polar** areas, when an orca finds a seal or bird near the edge of the ice, it sometimes dives deeply and then rushes up to the surface, breaking ice over a yard thick. The prey slides into the water, where the orca catches it.

This orca surges into shallow coastal waters to catch a sea lion in Argentina. Although orcas are often successful in catching prey this way, it can be a dangerous hunting method for them.

On to the beach

In Argentina orcas have learned to catch young elephant seals and sea lions on beaches by sliding up into shallow water, catching their prey, and then wriggling back into the sea. Orcas also use this dramatic method when hunting young seals around the Crozet Archipelago. Sometimes orcas accidentally beach themselves in the shallow water and die when hunting like this. When their heavy weight is no longer supported by water, their internal organs start to fail. If beached out of the water, their skin begins to dry out.

Another type of surprise attack is used to catch seals sitting on sheets of floating ice. A group of orcas moves forward quickly, making a huge wave that splashes over the ice and throws the seal into the water. Sometimes orcas simply use their heads to tilt up a floating ice sheet and attack the penguins or seals that fall into the water.

Orcas use other ways of finding food. In the seas around New Zealand, orcas search the shallow, coastal waters for large, flat fish called rays that live on the ocean floor. Around Alaska, and in the Indian Ocean, orcas sometimes steal fish that have been trapped on long fishing lines set by people.

Herding fish

Many **cetaceans,** including orcas, catch fish by herding. The orcas swim around and around a school of fish, guiding them up to the water's surface. They confuse the fish by flashing the white of their bellies. Once the school is tightly grouped, orcas take turns to dart in and seize mouthfuls of fish.

Learning the ropes

Female orcas are probably responsible for teaching hunting techniques to their offspring. For example, young orcas have been seen following their mothers as they attack seal pups near the shore.

*This orca is hunting a school of herring in waters off Norway by herding them together. Sometimes orcas slap the fish with their tail **flukes** to stun the fish.*

Into the deep

While diving, orcas can save their oxygen and slow down their heartbeat so less blood circulates through the body. The blood is then pushed to the brain and lungs where it is most needed. Orcas dive to depths of 98 to 213 feet (30 to 65 meters) in the wild in order to hunt. The deepest recorded orca dive reached 899 feet (274 meters).

Orcas are among the most exciting **cetaceans** to watch because of their fast, unpredictable movements and inquisitive behavior. Orcas can be very acrobatic. Some activities seem to have a definite purpose, but scientists do not understand the reasons for all of them. The orcas might just be having fun!

Orca tricks

Orcas frequently poke their heads vertically out of the water and get a good look around before slipping back silently below the surface. Sometimes a few orcas in a group do this together. This behavior is known as spy hopping. It is thought that orcas are either locating their **prey** or trying to confuse it.

This orca is spy hopping among the ice in the Ross Sea near Antarctica. Other cetaceans, such as pilot whales and gray whales, are also known to spy hop.

Orcas often swim upward at very fast speeds toward the surface so they can jump right out of the water, before landing again with a huge splash. This is called breaching and may be a way of communicating with each other. It may help loosen skin **parasites,** or just be another way of playing.

Tail slapping, or lob tailing, is another favorite orca activity. Orcas do this by sticking their tail **flukes** out of the water and slapping them down hard on the water's surface. It may be used as a warning sign to the rest of the group. The **pectoral fins** can also be raised out of the water and slapped noisily against the surface. When there are many whale watching boats present in Puget Sound, people have seen mother orcas with young slapping the water repeatedly.

▲ *Orcas are famous for their spectacular displays out of the water, especially breaching, where they leap clear of the surface and land on their back or side.*

In black and white

The striking black-and-white patterns on the skins of orcas play an important role, particularly when hunting. First, the bold coloring makes it hard for prey to recognize the complete shape of orcas in the water—a feature that scientists call disruptive coloration because it disrupts, or confuses, the whale's shape.

Second, orcas are countershaded. This means that they are mainly dark in color on top and light below. Any prey swimming above an orca might not be able to tell it apart from the blackness of the water below. Likewise, an animal swimming below an orca might look up to see the white orca belly against the light color of the sky. Either way, the orca's skin patterns help it to hide in the water when hunting.

Breeding

Orcas can **breed** at any time of the year, although in northern waters mating is most frequent from May to July. Scientists think that male orcas leave their family groups, or **pods,** for a time to seek out females from other pods in order to mate. Young orcas are called calves.

By swimming close to its mother and often in her wake—the disturbed area of water behind her—an orca calf can keep up with the pod using the minimum amount of energy.

Orca calves

The calf takes around seventeen months to develop inside its mother, and births usually take place in fall. Male orcas probably never meet their offspring, and do not seem to have any part in helping to raise them.

Like all young **cetaceans,** the orca calf is born underwater. Within seconds of its birth, the newborn animal swims to the surface for its first breath of air, helped by its mother's flippers. Within half an hour the calf can swim confidently. A newborn orca calf is around 6.5 feet (2 meters) long and weighs about 330 pounds (150 kilograms).

Growing up

Although male and female calves grow at a similar rate until they are around ten years old, the male orca eventually grows larger than the female orca.

Orca birth rates

Female orcas cannot breed until they are six to ten years old. They continue to produce calves every four to five years for the next twenty years. Twins are rare, but have been seen in the wild. Males mature later than females and are able to breed at between twelve and sixteen years of age. This low **birth rate** means that orca **populations** take a long time to recover from a decline in numbers, especially since half of newborn orcas die in their first year.

Like other **mammals,** the calf feeds on its mother's milk, suckling at one of her two teats. The creamlike milk is very rich and is up to 48 percent fat, so the calf can grow a thick, warm layer of **blubber** as quickly as possible. The calf begins to eat some solid food at three to four months old, but may be nursed by its mother for up to two years. Young calves eat herring, young salmon, and squid, when available.

The calf swims close to the mother. Keeping close like this makes it more difficult for a large shark to single the young orca out as **prey.** When the calf begins to communicate, it uses sounds similar to the calls of its mother.

Calves of **resident** orcas will spend their entire lives with their pod, swimming, hunting, and feeding alongside their mother, sisters, brothers, cousins, aunts, uncles, grandmother, and sometimes even great-grandmother.

An orca calf may stay very close to its mother, learning from her constantly, for up to ten years.

Toxic Chemicals in the Ocean

Humans have created around 80,000 new chemicals in the last 50 years. These **synthetic** chemicals have **contaminated** the air, rivers, and oceans all over the world. Even remote regions, like the Arctic, are now polluted by dangerous **toxic** chemicals that have arrived there through the air and by water.

The chemicals

PCBs (polychlorinated biphenyls) were invented in 1929 and used to cool and lubricate electrical equipment. In 1977 PCBs were banned in Canada, the United States, Europe, and Australia because they are so poisonous. However, by that time PCBs had already been dumped into the waters worldwide. PCBs are dangerous because they can damage the nervous system, and the development of young animals, including orcas. Humans are still pouring many other poisonous substances into the world's oceans, such as **pesticides** like DDT and **crude oil.** DDT can cause death to animals by poisoning. It can also cause various cancers and may interfere with **breeding.**

Long-lasting poisons

Chemicals like PCBs and DDT do not disappear quickly once put into the ocean, but remain in the environment for a long time, poisoning the water over many years.

This ship is discharging waste into Pearl Harbor, Hawaii. The illegal dumping of poisonous waste from ships is still a big environmental problem around the world.

Oil spills often mean disaster for wildlife and the environment. Here, people clean up oil that has washed up onto a beach following the Exxon Valdez accident in Alaska in 1989.

Problems in the food chain

Toxic chemicals and substances such as lead and mercury cause big problems in the oceans' **food chains.** The animals that live in the ocean take in these poisons with their food. Because the poisons are stored in their body fat, they get passed on as one animal eats another. As a **predator** at the top of the food chain, the orca receives very high levels of these **pollutants** through its food. They are also passed on to young whales as they develop inside their mothers' bodies, and later, too, through their mothers' milk.

Another **species** of whale, called the beluga, has recently been closely studied in Canada. Scientists found that PCBs in their bodies had lowered their **birth rate,** and made them more likely to catch diseases. Recent tests carried out off the state of Washington have shown that orcas there have four to five times more of these harmful PCBs in their bodies than the belugas in the Canadian study. This makes them some of the most contaminated animals on Earth.

Disaster at sea

On a clear, sunny day in March 1989, the *Exxon Valdez* oil tanker grounded. It spilled crude oil into the waters of Prince William Sound off Alaska. There was a lot of damage to wildlife. Some species, such as the harbor seal, still show little or no sign of recovery. From 1989 to 1990, one orca **pod** living in the area suddenly decreased in number from 36 to 22 whales. No young orcas were born in the pod immediately after the oil spill. Since 1995 numbers in the pod have been slowly rising again, reaching 26 orcas in 2001.

Noise Pollution and Boats

Orcas, like other **cetaceans,** have very sensitive hearing and live in a world full of sound. Even without human activities, the ocean can be a surprisingly noisy place. The moans and hums made by blue whales, for example, are the loudest noises made by any creature on Earth. They carry for thousands of miles across the oceans. Fish and **marine mammals** make a variety of sounds, and even heavy rain adds to the noise levels underwater.

These orcas have surfaced alongside an oil refinery in New Zealand. Oil rigs and oil exploration make a lot of underwater noise.

Humans have added greatly to underwater noise levels in recent years. Large ships, tankers, and speedboats are some of the main causes of increased noise in the ocean. Drilling for oil, exercises by military boats, and seal scarers that fishermen use to keep seals away from their nets also help to create what is called **noise pollution.** Scientists now believe that noise pollution is affecting the **echolocation** signals that cetaceans use to communicate with each other and locate their **prey.**

Noisy waters

Because orcas use sound to find and catch their prey, too much noise underwater forces them to swim harder and longer to find their prey, using up more energy. Eventually they need to make use of the energy stored in the layer of fat, called **blubber,** under their skin. Studies on whales in Puget Sound have found that they are now using nearly twenty percent more energy than they did before whale watching became popular there.

Whale watchers

Whale watching boats take people out to sea to watch whales for pleasure. However, these boats can also cause noise pollution and other problems for the orcas. They interfere with their hunting, resting, and family activities Sometimes large numbers of boats go out to watch the same group of whales. For example, in Puget Sound, there are often up to 100 whale watching boats out at the height of the season. Orcas also face the danger of being hit by boats or their propellers—this can cause serious injury or even death. A large number of orcas in New Zealand waters have suffered in this way.

Modern hunting

In Greenland people now use motorboats instead of canoes for seal hunting. It is possible that the decline in orcas in this area over recent years has been caused in part by the noise pollution these boats produce.

If whale watching boats get too close or approach too fast, they can cause orcas unnecessary stress and harm.

Smelly fumes

When there are many boats, exhaust fumes can collect over the surface of the water. When orcas come up to take a breath of fresh air, they take in smelly exhaust fumes instead. The effects of breathing polluted air have not been scientifically studied in orcas, but this must be very unhealthy for them.

Food Shortages

Human activities are reducing the types of food that orcas and other **marine predators** like to eat. Chinook salmon are a major part of the **diet** of **resident** orcas off the coast of the state of Washington. Recently their numbers have declined, partly because people are taking too many fish from the water. This is called **overfishing.**

As in other developed parts of the world, people living in Washington need more and more energy and water (energy to run streetlights and computers, and water to wash cars, water the grass, or take baths). To cope with the demand, large dams have been built across the rivers to generate **hydroelectric power.** In 2001, a drought year, the cities used up so much of the water from the rivers that 1.6 million young salmon were beached and died, and 150,000 fish had to be rescued.

Changes in the food chain

In the Crozet Archipelago in the Indian Ocean, the orca's main **prey** are southern elephant seals and **baleen** whales. In the past, human hunting of whales here caused baleen whale **populations** to drop, and they have not recovered. The population of elephant seals here also declined between 1970 and 1990, and remains at a low level. Here again, orcas are facing a shortage of food.

*Dams, like this one in the state of Washington, can prevent salmon from swimming upstream to **breed.** Fewer breeding salmon means less food for predators such as orcas.*

Changes in the **food chain** are affecting orcas in Alaska and the Aleutian Islands. Here seals and sea lions are an important part of the orca's diet, but their numbers are falling. In 1977 a sudden rise in water temperatures in the Gulf of Alaska led to a reduction in **plankton** and the animals that feed on them. This had a harmful effect further up the food chain, resulting in declines in the numbers of seals and sea lions, meaning less food for orcas.

Hungry orcas

When orcas are hungry and lack food, they begin to use their **blubber** reserves as food. In doing so, they release any poisons that may be present into their bloodstream. Along with the food shortages themselves, this is another threat to orcas today.

Overfishing of salmon off the coasts of North America, such as in Alaska, is causing food shortages for orcas.

Increase in fishing

Commercial fishing is now seriously affecting food chains in the ocean. Since the 1970s fishers have dramatically increased the number of fish they catch. The number of commercial fishing boats worldwide has doubled since 1970 and fishing techniques have become more destructive. As much as 25 percent of the fish caught are just thrown away because they are too small or of no commercial value. Many fish **species** are greatly reduced in numbers by overfishing, and predators, such as orcas, have less and less food.

Whaling and Orcas

Humans have used whale meat and oil from whale **blubber** for many centuries. Orcas were once hunted on a small scale by **native** peoples on the west coast of the United States. This is called **subsistence** hunting and still takes place in Greenland and Papua New Guinea in the southwest Pacific Ocean. Because only small numbers of whales are killed in subsistence hunting, it does not have a serious effect on whale **populations.**

A ban on whaling?

In 1946 the International Whaling Commission was set up to control whaling. In 1986 commercial whaling was banned. However, despite this ruling, Norway and Japan still continue to hunt whales commercially, although they do not take as many whales as in the past. Iceland started whaling again in 2003.

Commercial whaling, on the other hand, is whale hunting carried out to make money. Since its boom time around 1900, whaling has led to massive falls in the numbers of whales of different **species** around the world.

▲ *A minke whale is hauled aboard a whaling boat in the Barents Sea, Norway. Minke whales are among the most hunted whale species today.*

Meat and oil

Whales are hunted commercially for their meat and oil. Because orcas are not as big as other whales, they have not really been hunted commercially for their oil (21 orcas are needed to produce as much oil as 1 sperm whale, for example). However, orcas have been hunted in several regions around the world for their meat. For example, Norwegian whalers killed around 56 orcas each year from 1938 to 1981. In the 1979 to 1980 whaling season, the Soviet Union killed over 900 orcas in the Antarctic. Orcas are still killed today by whalers when they are hunting other species.

Conflict with fishers

Fishers have often killed or mistreated orcas because they thought that whales competed for the fish they were trying to catch. This led to many orca deaths in the Iceland and Norway herring fisheries. The killing of orcas by fishers is still a serious problem, particularly where orcas take fish straight from fishing nets, such as in Alaska. Fishers in the Crozet Archipelago in the Indian Ocean use illegal explosives to frighten away orcas from their fishing nets and lines.

Whale products

For centuries whales have been hunted for their oil and meat. Some of the uses for whale products have included margarine and cooking oil (from whale oil), corsets and umbrellas (from whalebone or **baleen**), fertilizer (from whale bones), and string for tennis racquets (from whale tendons). The sperm whale was hunted for a special kind of oil found in its head. This was used in lamp oil, as well as in candles, soaps, cosmetics, and perfume.

Beached Orcas

Beach rescue

Efforts are being made in some countries, including the United Kingdom, the United States, Argentina, and New Zealand, to rescue live beached cetaceans. Efforts are also being made to examine the bodies of dead animals that have washed ashore, to find out the cause of death. Beached animals can provide important information to scientists.

Every year thousands of whales, dolphins, and porpoises are found beached on coasts around the world. Some **cetaceans** die at sea and are washed up onto the shore. Others become trapped in shallow waters. Cetaceans may be washed ashore alone or in groups—these are known as mass beachings. Cetaceans beached on the shore usually die within a few hours or days if not given help.

Orca beachings are not as common as those of some other **species,** such as sperm whales, which are beached frequently, often in groups. Usually it is male orcas that are beached, although the reason for this is unknown. New Zealand has one of the highest rates of orca beaching in the world. Over 70 have been beached there since 1860, and in recent years there has been a beaching every 2 years on average. The high rate of live orca beachings in New Zealand may be a result of the whales' appetite for rays that live in the shallow waters there. Orcas are also frequently beached on the Argentine coast when chasing **prey,** such as sea lions, onto the shore.

This group of long-finned pilot whales has become beached. Rescuers help them by keeping them wet and covering their skin to prevent sunburn.

Helping a beached cetacean

If you find a beached whale or dolphin, it is important to call an expert for help as soon as possible. Many countries have networks of people who are specially trained in dealing with beached **marine mammals**. Always keep other people and dogs away from a beached cetacean to reduce stress to the animal.

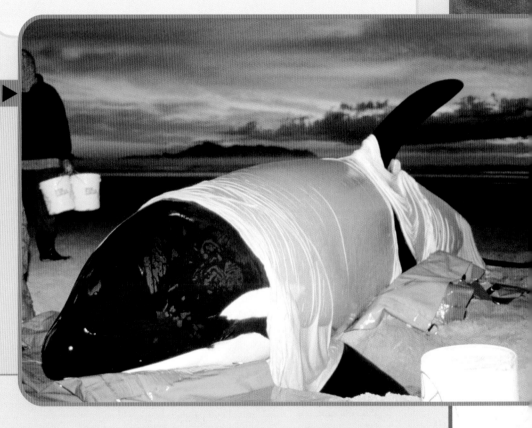

An orca has been left high and dry by the retreating tide on a New Zealand beach. A team of whale rescue volunteers in this country has saved the lives of thousands of cetaceans beached on the coast.

Live animals that have become beached alone are often old, injured, sick, or have lost their sense of direction. Mass beachings may occur because either the animal that is leading the rest of the group has made a mistake in **navigation** or has become sick or wounded and led the rest of its **pod** onto the shore. However, in many cases scientists do not know the reasons for the beachings, and many animals appear to be healthy. It is also not understood why beached whales that have been rescued and pulled back into deeper water will often immediately return to beach themselves again on the same stretch of shore.

Research and Protection

Because wild orcas spend almost their entire lives underwater, they are difficult to study. The dead bodies of whales provide valuable information for scientists. Some dead orcas are washed ashore, but most sink to the ocean floor and are never seen again.

Learning everything we can about orcas so that we can understand them better is one of the best ways to protect them and plan their **conservation.** Scientists are now studying them closely to try and find out, for example, why half of all newborn orcas die in their first year, whether increased boat traffic is seriously affecting whale behavior, and exactly how **toxic** chemicals are affecting their health.

*This leaping orca has a colored radio tag attached to its back behind its **dorsal fin.** These tags are important in whale research and can record information such as swimming speed and diving depths.*

Tagging orcas

One of the methods used to research and record orca behavior is the time-depth recording tag. Scientists attach these tags to beached orcas before they are returned to the ocean. The tags can provide valuable information. The tags are made to drop off after a while and float to the water's surface. A tag found on a beach in the state of Washington had been fixed to a male orca beached nearby two weeks earlier. The tag had recorded the orca's swimming speed, the depth to which it had been diving, and how often it surfaced, all of which indicated that it was doing well.

Well-studied orcas

Having been studied for 30 years, the northern and southern **resident** orcas off the west coast of the United States are among the best-researched whales in the world. Research programs have also been carried out on orcas in the Crozet Archipelago in the Indian Ocean, as well as in New Zealand and Argentina.

A **pod** of orcas swims near a whale research boat off the Lofoten Islands in Norway. Research into orca **populations** and behavior is very important for their future.

Orca protection

Orcas are listed as conservation dependent by the World Conservation Union. This is the international conservation group that is responsible for listing all plant and animal **species** that are thought to be at risk. *Conservation dependent* means that the orcas are the focus of a special conservation program. If this program is stopped, the species would be listed as threatened within five years, and the future survival of the species would be at risk.

Radio Orca!

Researchers have discovered a great deal of information about orca communication by listening to the sounds they make. Underwater sounds can be heard and recorded using a special underwater microphone, called a hydrophone. In Johnstone Strait, British Columbia, on the Canadian coast, the world's first whale radio station, ORCA-FM, was launched in July 1998. The whistles, whines, and squeals made by the orcas moving through the strait can be heard live 24 hours a day within several miles of this radio station.

How Sightings Can Help Orcas

These researchers are carrying out whale survey work. Although cetaceans may often be found in the same waters year round, they are usually easiest to find on calm days in clear, sunny weather.

Observing whales from the shore or from boats and gathering scientific information about them is an important part of whale research. Information such as which whale **species** was seen, how many whales, what they were doing, and where the sighting took place is all noted down. Whale sighting is different from whale watching: whale sightings gather important information, while whale watching is usually organized for groups of tourists.

Value to research?

Sightings of **cetaceans,** including orcas, off the coasts of the United States, Canada, Europe, Australia, and New Zealand are increasing as more people are becoming aware of whales and dolphins and are looking out for them.

Every reported sighting, whether it is from land or from a boat, can be valuable to whale scientists. The information from sightings is gathered together and put into computers. Building an accurate picture of orca movements helps scientists to find out how many whales there are in an area, and where they are in the world's oceans.

Orca dorsal fins

male   female

Male or female?

You can tell whether an orca is a male or female quite easily by the shape and size of its dorsal fin. The male's dorsal fin can be as tall as a human—about 6 feet (almost 2 meters) high—and is the tallest dorsal fin in the animal kingdom. It is more upright and triangular than the female's dorsal fin, which is usually about 4 feet (1.2 meters) high, and curved backward.

Identifying orcas

With their distinctive black-and-white patterning, huge, rounded head and tall **dorsal fin,** orcas are easy to spot when they emerge from the water. Even if they only surface partly, you can usually see the dorsal fin and shape of the head. Another helpful feature for recognizing orcas is the shape of the blow, or spout—the cloud of moist air that whales breathe out from their blowholes.

Scientists can easily identify individual orcas by using photographs. Each orca has a light gray patch behind the dorsal fin, known as a saddle patch. It is different in shape and size in every animal. Orcas usually also have scars or nicks on the dorsal fins or distinctive white eye patches. These features are photographed and cataloged and can be used by scientists to follow individual orcas throughout their lives.

An orca's blow is a fine spray about ten feet (three meters) in height, and wide and rounded in shape, rather like a bush. It often makes an explosive sound, and is a useful way of recognizing orcas in the water.

Reducing Toxic Chemicals

In our daily lives we depend on the use of hundreds of different **synthetic** chemicals—for example in plastics, cosmetics, cleaners, food preservatives, **pesticides,** and even computers.

Some of these chemicals are very poisonous to wildlife and also to ourselves. For example, PCBs were once thought to be harmless, but even though they have been banned they are still having harmful effects on animals, including orcas, around the world.

Even beaches on remote islands are often littered with trash, sometimes brought long distances by ocean currents.

Do not be a litter bug!

The litter we drop on beaches, particularly plastics and soda cans, can harm marine wildlife if they try to eat it or get tangled up in it. When having a party outside, keep all balloons carefully tied down. If they float away, eventually they will end up as trash on land or in the water, where they may be mistakenly swallowed by animals.

Action needed!

Conservation groups believe the risks to the environment—our land, rivers, oceans, and the air we breathe—are so high that we should all take action now to reduce our use of **toxic** chemicals. Conservation groups, like the World Wildlife Fund (WWF), are campaigning for new laws that will stop the use of long-lasting chemicals. To reduce the threat from toxic chemicals, governments and the public all over the world will need to play a part. The good news is that it is possible to reverse the damaging effects of these chemicals over time.

Making a difference

We can all do something to help. We can avoid the use of pesticides in the home and yard, for example, and use cleaning products that do not harm the environment. We can buy soap, shampoos, and cosmetics that do not contain synthetic perfumes, and use paints, varnishes, and glues that are based on water and not synthetic chemicals. Organic farming avoids the use of harmful chemicals, such as pesticides, and is gentle on the environment. You can find out more about this from organic farming groups.

It is a good idea to find out where your water comes from and where it goes once you have used it. Never pour any paints or synthetic chemicals down the drain. **Pollutants** can travel down to the ocean through our rivers and streams, and have harmful effects on **marine** life. If you are unsure about what to do with any dangerous or poisonous waste, contact your local environmental agencies.

We can all help to clean up litter on our beaches. Here children are keeping a record of the garbage they have collected on a beach in the United Kingdom.

Protecting Food Supplies

Our own huge demands for water and energy, along with the practice of **overfishing,** are all affecting the orca's food supply. Off the coast of the state of Washington, for example, chinook salmon have been decreasing in numbers. This leaves orcas with little of their main source of food.

Water and energy

Conservation groups in Washington are now encouraging people to reduce their use of water and energy in order to restore the river levels and the salmon numbers. Over a quarter of all water used in a typical house is used just to flush toilets! Bathing accounts for the third largest use of indoor water and the second highest use of energy in the Washington survey. There are now water-saving devices that can help reduce the amount of water used in toilets, washing machines, and showers.

Of course, it is important to preserve water and cut down on the energy we use wherever we live. It all adds up to help the environment. Advice on how to make homes more energy efficient and how to insulate them better is often free from energy supply companies. Putting weather strips around doors and windows, for example, helps plug leaks and prevents the escape of heat energy. Replacing standard light bulbs with compact fluorescent bulbs also saves large amounts of energy. Water heaters that use **solar power** to provide hot water can cut the use of **hydroelectric power.**

These steps were built for fish! This is a fish ladder in Oregon, built next to a large dam. The ladder enables salmon in the river to bypass the dam and continue their journey upstream to **breed.**

A salmon leaps out of the water to try to escape a hunting orca. Here, off the Canadian coast, the salmon are plentiful and there is a healthy orca population.

Helping the salmon

People are now working hard to restore salmon **habitat** along the rivers in Washington by planting trees and shrubs along the riverbanks. This will provide better shade, reduce water temperature, and prevent banks from collapsing, making the rivers more suitable for salmon to **breed.** It all helps orca **conservation,** too. Fishers are being encouraged to give up fishing for salmon altogether, or at least avoid fishing in **Marine** Protected Areas, where fish **populations** are being helped to recover.

Salmon and orcas

Salmon are remarkable fish. They are born in freshwater streams. They swim down to the ocean to mature, and eventually return to the same stream where they were born, to breed. They may travel as far as 1,000 miles (nearly 1,600 kilometers) from the ocean to the river to lay their eggs, after which they usually die. During the years that they spend maturing in the ocean, salmon born in Washington travel thousands of miles all around the northern Pacific Ocean from Washington to Alaska, Japan, and Russia. Orcas catch salmon in coastal waters either soon after they leave their freshwater streams when young, or as they return to breed.

Whale Watching and Orcas

Commercial whale watching for pleasure began in the 1950s. Today there are many companies that offer tourists the chance to watch whales and dolphins in the wild all over the world. Trips on whale watching boats can last just one hour or up to two weeks.

Harm or help?

Whale watching can cause harm to whales if there are too many boats, or if it is done carelessly, since **cetaceans** can then suffer from **noise pollution,** or may even collide with boats. This has happened on some trips around San Juan Island in Puget Sound.

On the other hand, if carried out responsibly, whale watching can help orca **conservation** through the interest it creates in people. Whale watching provides fantastic opportunities to see these animals in the wild. Since the orca is a particularly spectacular, active, and acrobatic **species,** it is very popular with whale watchers.

Spot the orca! Children watch orcas from the deck of a whale watching boat off the coast of the state of Washington. Their boat is keeping away from the orcas in order not to upset them.

A whale watching trip is an unforgettable experience. Educational talks and commentaries during the trips help to raise people's awareness, and inspire them to help care for the **marine** environment and the wildlife, such as orcas, that live there. Whale watch operators in many parts of the world are also in a good position to carry out valuable research.

Big business

Whale watching is a booming business. The industry is worth millions of dollars in Iceland. Income from whale watching has become important to coastal communities such as Provincetown in Massachusetts, Tofino in British Columbia, Canada, and Monkey Mia in Australia. The benefit to whales is that responsible whale watching makes money from these animals without harming them. This means that if whales are properly protected, whale watching can provide people in coastal communities with a good, long-term income.

*Whale researchers use whale watching boat trips to carry out their orca studies. The shape of the **dorsal fins** is often used to help identify individual orcas.*

Whale Watching Code of Conduct

This is the whale and dolphin watching code of conduct and should be followed by all whale watching boat operators:

- Keep your distance. Never go closer than 325 feet (100 meters) or 650 feet (200 meters) if another boat is present.
- Never drive head on to, or move between, scatter, or separate cetaceans. If unsure of their movements, simply stop and put the engine into neutral.
- Spend no longer than 15 minutes near the animals.
- Take special care with mothers and young.
- Maintain a steady direction and keep speeds low.
- Never try to swim with wild cetaceans, for your safety and theirs.
- Do not dispose of any garbage or litter in the water.

Orcas in Marine Parks

Whales and dolphins, including orcas, are kept in **marine** parks and aquariums around the world. Most sea **mammals** in captivity, including orcas, have been taken from the wild. Over 130 orcas have been captured for aquariums and marine parks since 1961. Waters off the northwest coast of the United States and off Iceland once provided many orcas for this purpose, before the capture of live orcas was banned. Some orcas have been caught recently in Japanese waters for marine parks in Japan, and the Russian government gave permission to catch 10 live orcas off its east coast in 2003.

Problems of live capture

Scientists do not yet fully understand the effects of capture upon wild **populations** of orcas, or upon individual animals. Capturing a mother orca will affect young that still depend on her. Removing a young orca means the **pod** has lost an animal that can **breed** in the future, and this may harm the pod, since orcas have such low **birth rates.**

Scientists believe that whales can become stressed during capture and when transported. In nature the orca is a wild animal that lives in groups and swims in open waters. In captivity an orca's surroundings are very different. It is confined in a small space near noisy humans, and since hunting real **prey** is no longer possible, it is given dead fish to eat.

After capture, orcas become tame and can easily be taught to perform tricks and spectacular acrobatics for the crowds.

Keiko's story

Keiko was captured by fishers in Icelandic waters in 1979 when he was two years old. In captivity he became a performing animal, and in 1992 he starred in the popular movie, *Free Willy*. When people found out about his poor health and living conditions, Keiko was moved to an aquarium in the United States for two years. He was brought back to good health. Once he was healthy, Keiko went to an enclosure on the Icelandic coast where the staff began to prepare him for release back into the wild. When released in 2002, he swam from Iceland to Norway, where he became so popular that he had to be moved to a more remote bay. He was fed there, but he was free to roam. Sadly, in December 2003, Keiko suddenly became ill and died.

Benefits to orcas?

Until around 25 years ago, orcas were widely feared and misunderstood. Watching these whales in captivity has improved the orca's image among the public. Orcas are now widely appreciated as intelligent animals, rather than cruel **predators.** Seeing orcas up close is an experience that most people would never be able to enjoy otherwise. Many people also think that marine parks can have a valuable educational role.

Keiko's capture and release into the wild were very controversial and many people have mixed feelings about it.

How Can You Help?

Orcas are facing many serious threats today all over the world, and the task of helping them may seem very difficult. In fact there is a lot you can do to help.

Adopt an orca

Try taking part in an adopt-a-whale program. By adopting an orca, you will be helping to support research of orcas in the wild that is vital for their **conservation.** There are several programs: the Adopt a Whale Program run by the Whale and Dolphin Conservation Society, the Orca Adoption Program in the United States, the B.C. Wild Killer Whale Adoption Program in Canada, or the Adopt an Orca projects in the United States and New Zealand. You can often choose the orca you want to adopt from photographs online. In return you will receive a photograph of your whale and be kept up-to-date with all the latest news on orca research.

Take part!

You can also get involved by joining a whale conservation organization and actively taking part in their campaigns. You will receive regular newsletters or magazines letting you know about the organization's work and updates on whale conservation. You may be able to participate in interesting events. Try emailing or writing letters to your elected government representatives about the threats to orcas. They will listen to your concerns about important conservation issues.

Adopting a whale is a great way to help conserve orcas and other whales. You can find out more about adopting whales by contacting conservation groups.

High numbers of orcas are a sign that our oceans are healthy. Helping to conserve whales is not only good for them, it benefits our environment and local communities, too.

Whale sightings

Taking part in whale sighting programs is also of great value to orca research. Programs are organized by the Whale and Dolphin Conservation Society, Adopt an Orca, and the Whale Museum. Whale watching tours are among the most exciting wildlife experiences on Earth! There are opportunities to take part in the United Kingdom, the United States, Australia, New Zealand, and in many other countries around the world. Just make sure your boat operator follows the whale watching code. Then you can really enjoy watching orcas and other **cetaceans,** too, and learn more about these wonderful animals.

Read on

You can find out much more about the fascinating world of orcas and other cetaceans, and the threats to their survival, by looking for information on the Internet and reading books.

Glossary

baleen   comblike structure in a whale's mouth made of keratin that filters food from the water

birth rate   number of young produced by an animal over a fixed time period

blubber   layer of fat under the skin of marine mammals

breed   produce young

cetacean   mammal that spends its entire life in water. Cetaceans need to come to the surface regularly to breathe air, and have one or two nostrils, or blowholes.

commercial   done to make money

conservation   work done to protect wild plants and animals and their habitats

contaminate   pollute

crude oil   oil that has not yet been purified for use

diet   food an animal eats

dorsal fin   fin located on the back of a fish or whale

echolocation   detection of objects using high-frequency sound waves, used by some animals, including orcas, to locate prey or find their way about

ecosystem   all the plants and animals in an area together with their nonliving environment

endothermic   warm-blooded, maintaining a more or less constant body temperature that is largely independent of the temperature of the environment

estuary   river mouth, where fresh water and ocean water meet

fluke   broad flat tail fin of cetaceans

food chain   series of living things, each forming food (and so providing energy) for the next living thing in the chain

habitat   place where a plant or animal naturally lives

hydroelectric power   energy generated from the power of falling water in rivers or streams

mammal   warm-blooded animal that feeds its young with milk from its body

marine   living in the ocean. Marine parks are wildlife parks where marine animals are kept.

mucus   slimy, slippery substance produced by some living organisms

native   belonging to a particular country or place

navigation   method of finding out where you are on land or water

noise pollution   sound that is harmful to humans or wildlife

nutrient   substance that provides nourishment

overfishing   taking too many fish from the ocean

parasite   animal that lives on or inside another animal's body. Large numbers can cause illness.

pectoral fin   side fin

pesticide   substance that kills pests, such as wasps and flies, and is usually human made

plankton   tiny forms of life that live in the seas, lakes, and rivers

pod   social group of whales

polar   area within the Arctic or Antarctic Circles

pollutant   substance that causes pollution

pollution   presence of high levels of harmful substances in the environment, often put there by human activity

population   group of living things of the same species within a particular area

predator   animal that hunts or kills another animal for food

prey   animal hunted or killed by another animal for food

resident   living in one place. Resident orcas stay in one area in close family groups.

solar power   energy from the Sun

species   particular type of animal or other living thing. Orcas are a species of whale.

subsistence   what is needed to support life

synthetic   not naturally occurring, but made by humans

toxic   poisonous

transient   not living in one place all the time

tropical   climate that is moist and very warm

Conservation groups

American Cetacean Society
Organization in the United States that works to protect whales, dolphins, and porpoises and their habitats through education, conservation, and research.

P.O. Box 1391
San Pedro, CA 90733-1391

The Whale Museum
62 First Street N
P.O. Box 945
Friday Harbor, WA

Whale Times
P.O.Box 2702
Tualatin, OR 97062

World Wildlife Fund (WWF)
The WWF is an international organization that takes action to protect threatened species and tackle global threats to the environment for the benefit of people and nature. The WWF has branches in many countries around the world.

1250 24th Street NW
Washington, DC 20037-1175

Books

Carwadine, Mark. *Killer Whale.* Chicago: Raintree, 2000.

Gentle, Victor and Janet Perry. *Orcas: Killer Whales.* Milwaukee: Gareth Stevens, 2001.

Morgan, Sally. *Mammals.* Chicago: Raintree, 2005.

Solway, Andrew. *Classifying Mammals.* Chicago: Heinemann Library, 2003.

Spilsbury, Louise and Richard Spilsbury. *A Pod of Whales.* Chicago: Heinemann Library, 2003.

Stefanow, Jennifer. *Polluted Waters.* Chicago: Raintree, 2004.

Index